Animal
High Jumping Stars

BY SUSAN E. HAMEN

The Child's World®
childsworld.com

Published by The Child's World®
1980 Lookout Drive • Mankato, MN 56003-1705
800-599-READ • www.childsworld.com

Photographs ©: Paul Bull/iStockphoto, cover, 1; Stephen Dalton/
Science Source, 5; Diego Barbieri/Shutterstock Images, 6; filip
bossuyt CC2.0, 7; Peggy Woods Ryan/Shutterstock Images, 9,
20; Nati Harnik/AP Images, 10; Rolf Nussbaumer/ImageBROKER
RM/Glow Images, 13, 21; Scott Linstead/Science Source, 14, 19;
iStockphoto, 17, 20–21

ISBN 9781503820401
LCCN 2016960510

Printed in the United States of America
PA02341

ABOUT THE AUTHOR

Susan E. Hamen has written more than 20 books for children and loves learning about new things when she writes. Her book *Clara Barton: Civil War Hero and American Red Cross Founder* was chosen for the American Library Association's 2011 Amelia Bloomer Project Book List. She lives in Minnesota with her husband, Ryan, and her two children, Maggie and Jack.

Contents

CHAPTER 1

High Jumping Stars

Boing! The animal world is filled with high jumpers. Some of these bouncy creatures are large. Others are very small. Some have fur and some have hair. Some even have scales and live in water!

Humans can jump high, too. Both animals and humans can jump distances as well as heights.

Some athletes compete against each other in the high jump. They run and jump. They throw their bodies over a crossbar. Then, they land safely on big cushions. Jumpers must have strong leg muscles to push high into the air. They must also be very flexible to arch their bodies over the bar. Jumpers cannot knock down the bar. If they do, their jump does not count. Each athlete jumps three times.

This red-eyed tree frog is jumping high for food.

There are two kinds of high jump competitions: indoor and outdoor.

The bar is raised a bit higher with each round of jumping. The winner is the jumper who can jump the highest without knocking the bar down.

In the 2016 Summer Olympics, Ruth Beitia from Spain won the gold medal for the women's high jump.

She was the oldest woman to win a gold medal in the sport. She was 37 years old. Her winning jump was 6.46 feet (1.97 m). That's about as tall as a professional male basketball player!

In this book, three of nature's best high jumpers will compete in the Animal Olympics. Which one will win the gold medal? Let's find out!

ATHLETE PROFILE
NAME: Ruth Beitia
BORN: April 1, 1979, in Santander, Spain
HEIGHT: 6.25 feet (192 cm)
WEIGHT: 157 pounds (71 kg)
HIGHEST JUMP: 6.63 feet (2.02 m) in 2007
RECORDS: 6.46-foot (1.97 m) jump; gold medal for the women's high jump in the 2016 Olympic Games

CHAPTER 2

The Rock-Jumping Klipspringer

The klipspringer is a small African antelope. It lives in the mountains of eastern and southern Africa. It has an unusual name. Klipspringer means "rock jumper" in the Afrikaans language. The klipspringer is approximately as tall as a red fox. It's a very small antelope, but it is the highest jumper for its size among mammals.

ANIMAL PROFILE
NAME: Klipspringer
HEIGHT: 1.6 feet (45 cm) tall at the shoulders
WEIGHT: 24 to 29 pounds (11 to 13 kg)
HIGHEST JUMP: 16 feet (5 m)

Klipspringers are often found walking on their tiptoes.

The klipspringer lives in rocky parts of the mountains. There, it eats flowers, tender green shoots, fruits, and shrubs. The small klipspringer must be aware of its **predators**, because it cannot fight them off. Leopards, jackals, eagles, and baboons **prey** upon the klipspringer.

When the klipspringer is threatened, it flees to higher rocks. When it senses danger, the klipspringer can jump 16 feet (5 m) into the air! It springs off the tips of its hooves to escape. The klipspringer leaps higher and higher up the mountain until it is safe. It can land on pieces of rock the size of a silver dollar. Its small round hooves grip the rocks tightly. It can jump to small rocks sticking out on the side of the mountain. There, it's safe from predators.

In some parts of Africa, only the male klipspringers have horns.

CHAPTER 3

The Bold Jumping Spider

The next high-jumping animal is the daring jumping spider. Also called the bold jumping spider, this spider is part of the largest spider species in the world. There are more than 5,000 kinds of jumping spiders. They are found all over the globe, but mostly in tropical areas. The daring jumping spider is the most common jumping spider in North America.

Daring jumping spiders are mostly black. They have eight eyes, including two on the back of their head!

ANIMAL PROFILE
NAME: Daring Jumping Spider
LENGTH: .24 to .75 inch (6 to 19 mm)
WEIGHT: Unknown
HIGHEST JUMP: 11 inches (300 mm)

Daring jumping spiders are known for their blue-green fangs.

Four sets of eyes allow daring jumping spider to see prey, or predators, up to 7 inches (20 cm) away.

Given its many eyes, the daring jumping spider has incredible eyesight. This is what the spider solely relies on to find prey because it doesn't have ears.

Fun Fact

Unlike most spiders, daring jumping spiders don't make webs to catch prey. They do, however, release a small line of webbing when they jump to catch them if they fall.

The daring jumping spider eats insects, including worms, stink bugs, and grasshoppers. It has strong **hind** legs. These legs help the spider sneak attack its prey. To hunt, the spider leaps on its prey and bites it, releasing venom into the victim. Some jumping spiders have been known to leap 50 times their body length! This would be like a human jumping nearly an entire football field in one leap!

CHAPTER 4

High-Hopping Tree Frog

The red-eyed tree frog is the final jumper. This small frog has bright lime-green skin. It also has yellow and blue stripes on its side. The frog's red eyes bulge out. The red-eyed tree frog is a colorful creature. It is also a high jumper.

The red-eyed tree frog lives in Central and South America. It stays in trees near rivers. It hides in the leaves and waits for insects. The tree frog eats crickets. It also eats grasshoppers and flies. It has a long, sticky tongue.

ANIMAL PROFILE
NAME: Red-Eyed Tree Frog
LENGTH: 1.5 to 3 inches (4 to 8 cm)
WEIGHT: .21 to .53 ounces (6 to 15 g)
HIGHEST JUMP: More than 5 feet (1.5 m)

The red-eyed tree frog is also called the monkey frog after its jumping abilities.

This helps the frog grip onto its prey. The red-eyed tree frog also has small **suction cups** on its toes. These help the frog cling to leaves. The frogs sleep during the day.

The red-eyed tree frog has many predators. Bats, owls, snakes, tarantulas, and young alligators all eat red-eyed tree frogs. When the tree frog senses danger, it opens its eyes. The large red eyes scare away some predators. If not, the tree frog uses its strong legs to jump far away. It can jump up 20 times its length in one leap! This mighty jumper doesn't even need a running start. Scientists use high-speed cameras to record jumping frogs. This allows them to learn a lot about the frog's jumping abilities.

The red-eyed tree frog's bright colors help keep it safe in the rainforest.

CHAPTER 5

The Award Ceremony

GOLD MEDAL
Klipspringer

SILVER MEDAL
Red-Eyed Tree Frog

Which would win in an Olympic-style high jump? The klipspringer wins the gold medal with its 16-foot (5 m) jump! The red-eyed tree frog springs into second place with its 5-foot (1.5 m) jump. The daring jumping spider can leap far, but not high. It comes in third place with the bronze medal. Congratulations to the athletes!

BRONZE MEDAL
Daring Jumping Spider

Glossary

hind (HYND) The hind is the back or rear of something. Jumping spiders have strong hind legs that help them leap far.

predators (PRED-uh-turs) Predators are animals that kill and eat other animals for food. The klipspringer leaps to safety to avoid predators.

prey (PRAY) Prey is an animal killed and eaten by another animal. Red-eyed tree frogs are prey for hungry bats.

suction cups (SUHK-shuhn KUHPS) Suction cups are disc-shaped objects that help something cling to a surface. The frog's toes have suction cups, which help it cling to the tree.

To Learn More

In the Library

Bowman, Chris. *Tree Frogs*. Minneapolis, MN:
Bellwether Media, 2015.

Lunis, Natalie. *Tricky Tree Frogs*.
New York, NY: Bearport Publishing, 2010.

Randolph, Joanne. *Jumping Spiders*.
New York, NY: Rosen Publishing, 2014.

On the Web

Visit our Web site for links about
high jumping animals: **childsworld.com/links**

Note to Parents, Teachers, and Librarians: We routinely verify our
Web links to make sure they are safe and active sites.
So encourage your readers to check them out!

Index